Read and Play! 1

Izzy the Bear

7

No Part of this publication may be reproduced, stored in a retrieval system, or transmitted in any form or my any means, electronic, mechanical, photocopying, recording, or otherwise without written permission of the publisher.

Copyright © 2013 T.S. Cherry
Editor: Brenda Walker
All rights reserved.
ISBN: 978-0-692-39597-4

Imprint Name: Pop Academy of Music

The Spaces of the Bass Clef

 First Space above the staff

 Fourth Space

 Third Space

 Second Space

 First Space

 First Space below the staff

4   6   1   3   5   7

Locate the **Spaces** piano key.

The Lines of the Bass Clef

 — Fifth Line

 — Fourth Line

 — Third Line

 — Second Line

 — First Line

 — First Line below the staff

3   5   7   2   4   6

Locate the **Lines** piano key.

Izzy the bear

Loves to entertain the young.

"When I grow up," he said,

"All I want to do is have fun."

He put on a wig

Balanced a toy on his nose.

All the keynotes giggles

As he lit fire to his toes.

"It's time for us to talk,"

His father would say.

"It's going to have to wait father I only have time to play."

"One day," his father warned
"You'll have to grow up,

Learn the business,

We're depending on you, grow up."

He put on his red wig

And a red nose he had found.

Then juggled for the kids

He loved being a clown.

"One day," his father warned
"You'll have to grow up,

Learn the business,

We're depending on you, grow up."

" Not now father
I have a show to prepare."

He attached his black tie
And waved his hands in the air.

"One day," his father warned,

"You'll have to grow up.

Learn the business,

We're depending on you, grow up."

Izzy couldn't understand

Why he wouldn't let it be.

"I like making people laugh

It's my duty, you see."

"Obligation is key,"

His father would say.

"Is this what you want them to remember
That you just up and walked away?"

"It's all anyone will remember

It's all anyone will see.

Haven't you noticed

How everyone depends on me?"

Off to class Izzy went

To make people laugh.

"It's just who I am," he thought,

"How can that make him sad?"

Izzy thought and he thought
He knew what his father said to be true.
"I have an obligation," he said
"However, I have a talent too."

Izzy thought and thought
Then came up with a plan.
"I'll be a clown that teaches music
Oh, yes I can."

Then he grabbed a set of balls

And juggled them in class.

"I am the space above

The bass clef staff," he said.

Seventh green key is my task."

" below middle C of the treble clef
I am the bear you see,

We are the Pola Bears, we live inside the large dragon tree."

His father paused as he listened

To the plans of his son.

Then he put on a smile

After he realized what he'd done.

"You are all grown up

Your first battle has been won."

You've learned to use your talent

To show everyone where we are from."

www.ingramcontent.com/pod-product-compliance
Lightning Source LLC
Chambersburg PA
CBHW072116290426
44110CB00014B/1930